Garden Birds

handbook

Garden Birds

handbook

Written by
Duncan Brewer

Illustrated by
Alan Harris

Miles Kelly
PUBLISHING

First published in 2003 by Miles Kelly Publishing Ltd,
Bardfield Centre, Great Bardfield, Essex, CM7 4SL

Copyright © Miles Kelly Publishing Ltd 2003

British Library Cataloguing-in-Publication Data
A catalogue record for this book is available from the
British Library

ISBN 1-84236-313-1

2 4 6 8 10 9 7 5 3

Project Manager: Kate Miles
Assistant: Carol Danenbergs
Design: Guy Rodgers
Production: Estela Godoy

Contact us by email: info@mileskelly.net
Website: www.mileskelly.net

Printed in China

Key

 Starlings and Thrushes

 Tits

 Finches

 Sparrows and Buntings

 Woodpeckers

 Owls

 Warblers

 Swifts, Swallows and Martins

 Wagtails, Flycatchers and Chats

 Pigeons and Doves

 Birds of Prey

 Gulls

 Crows

 Herons

 Game Birds

Contents

HOW TO USE THIS BOOK

Here are a few notes on finding your way round the pages of your bird guide. Read them and get started!

Place your 'I've seen it!' sticker here

Birdspotting record

Questions to help you successfully identify birds

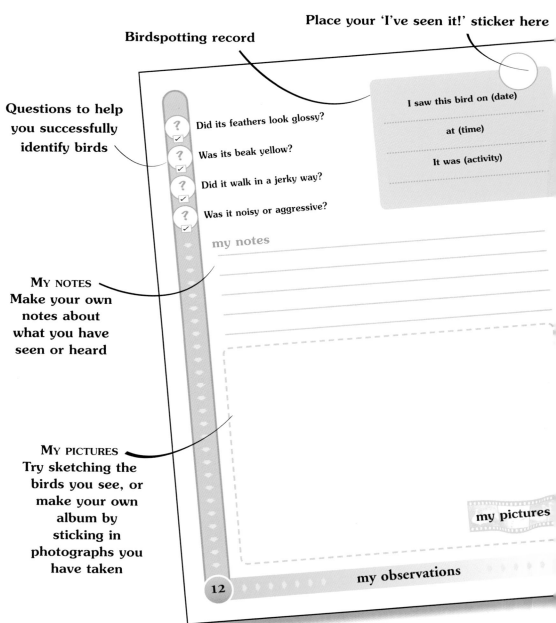

? ✓ Did its feathers look glossy?

? ✓ Was its beak yellow?

? ✓ Did it walk in a jerky way?

? ✓ Was it noisy or aggressive?

I saw this bird on (date)

at (time)

It was (activity)

my notes

MY NOTES
Make your own notes about what you have seen or heard

MY PICTURES
Try sketching the birds you see, or make your own album by sticking in photographs you have taken

my pictures

my observations

12

6

FOOD THAT BIRDS FIND FOR THEMSELVES

• A bird-friendly garden will have a good variety of shrubs and trees that can provide fruits and seeds, and also attract insects. Blackbirds and thrushes will forage through undergrowth and leaf litter for insects, as well as feeding on berries and fruits in the autumn. The scarlet berries of the rowan tree attract thrushes and starlings, and other good berry plants are hawthorn, elder, honeysuckle, ivy and yew.

• Several garden birds welcome rotting windfall apples and pears, pecking out the flesh and leaving the hollow skin.

• A patch of wild garden is a good idea. Clumps of nettles and brambles provide a treasure-trove of seeds, insects and caterpillars. Dead branches, or a pile of old logs, will also provide richpickings, especially for small birds like wrens that like to forage in dark places. Goldfinches will extract tiny seeds from teazels and thistles.

• Nest-boxes placed high in trees may attract birds such as blue tits and great tits, but even more attractive to these birds are natural nesting-sites such as ivy-covered walls, old trees and thick hedgerows.

• Finally, a pond with shallow fringes and a good supply of water plants will attract birds to drink, bathe and hunt insects.

? Did its feathers look glossy? ✓

? Was its beak yellow? ✓

? Did it walk in a jerky way? ✓

? Was it noisy or aggressive? ✓

I saw this bird on (date)

....

at (time)

....

It was (activity)

....

my notes

_____

_____

_____

_____

_____

my pictures

my observations

Common Starling (*Sturnus vulgaris*)

Once a woodland bird, the starling is now one of the commonest birds seen in towns and villages. Starlings are noisy and energetic birds, and a small flock can clear a bird-table of all food in a matter of seconds. Winter flocks flying to roost in town or country may number many thousands of birds, swooping and wheeling in unison, and chattering noisily once roosted. Enthusiastic bird-bath visitors, starlings dip and shake vigorously, then preen, spreading special oil from a rump gland over all their feathers before smoothing them back into shape.

JAN FEB MAR APR MAY JUN JUL AUG SEP OCT NOV DEC

6 = very common 0 = very rare

RESIDENT/VISITOR
Resident, with some winter visitors from northern Europe.

FACTS

SIZE	Length 22 cm Weight 75–90 g
COLOUR	MALE: Metallic sheen to most feathers, with pale feather tips. Light-brown edging to wing feathers. FEMALE: Similar to male. More light-brown on wing feathers in summer. WINTER DIFFERENCES: Bill turns yellow. Feather tips brighter after autumn moult.
NEST	Untidy straw, grass, feathers. Usually in a hole in trees, buildings, cliffs, nest-boxes.
CALL	Harsh 'tcheer'. Song – whistles, clicks and mimicry of other birds.

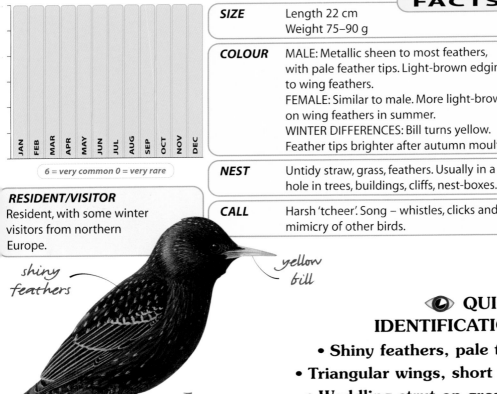

shiny feathers

yellow bill

♂

👁 QUICK IDENTIFICATION

- **Shiny feathers, pale tips**
- **Triangular wings, short tail**
- **Waddling strut on ground**
- **Often in flocks at dusk**

13

? ✓ Did it repeat its song phrase three or four times?

? ✓ Did it run and hop?

? ✓ Did you see evidence of smashed snail shells?

? ✓ Did it have a spotted breast?

I saw this bird on (date)
....

at (time)
....

It was (activity)
....

my notes

....

....

....

....

....

my pictures

my observations

Song Thrush *(Turdus philomelos)*

The song thrush is the most familiar of the garden 'spotted' thrushes. It can be seen, sometimes in pairs, moving in runs and hops as it hunts worms, snails and insects. Once more common than the blackbird, its numbers have fallen in recent years. A sure sign of a song thrush is a stone 'anvil', surrounded with the broken shells of the snails it has hammered open. As well as live food, the song thrush eats soft fruit and berries, and is particularly fond of yew berries. It is more likely to appear in the garden shrubbery than at the bird-table.

JAN FEB MAR APR MAY JUN JUL AUG SEP OCT NOV DEC

6 = very common 0 = very rare

RESIDENT/VISITOR
Mainly resident, though some migrate south.

FACTS

SIZE	Length 23 cm Weight 70–90 g
COLOUR	MALE: Brown back, buff underparts. Spotted breast. FEMALE: Same as male. WINTER DIFFERENCES: None.
NEST	Dried stems lined with mud and rotting wood, bound with saliva and drying hard. Trees, hedges, shed rafters.
CALL	Loud 'tchuk'. In flight – 'sip'. Song – flute-like repeated phrases.

slender bill

creamy-yellow and black spots

brown back

👁 QUICK IDENTIFICATION

- **Narrow breast spots**
- **Buff underwing visible in flight**
- **Brown cap and back**
- **Two- and three-note song, repeated several times**

15

? Was it larger than the song thrush?
☑

? Was its song similar to but faster than a blackbird's?
☑

? Did it have white patches under its wings?
☑

? Did it have a spotted breast?
☑

I saw this bird on (date)

....

at (time)

....

It was (activity)

....

my notes

my pictures

my observations

Mistle Thrush (*Turdus viscivorus*)

The mistle thrush is the largest British thrush. It is also known as the 'storm cock', because it sings from the treetops when winds are blowing hard. It forages on the ground for insects, worms and snails in spring and summer. It feeds on fruit and berries in winter, including yew, hawthorn, holly, mistletoe and ivy. Although usually nervous of humans, and uncommon at the bird-table, the mistle thrush can be very aggressive in the breeding season, even attacking dogs and gardeners. You can see it in most terrains, from gardens and orchards to woodland, moorland and other wild country.

JAN FEB MAR APR MAY JUN JUL AUG SEP OCT NOV DEC

6 = very common 0 = very rare

FACTS

SIZE	Length 27 cm Weight 110–140 g
COLOUR	MALE: Grey-brown upperparts, buff underparts, pure white underwing. Dark spotted breast. FEMALE: Similar to male. WINTER DIFFERENCES: None.
NEST	Grass, moss, reinforced with earth, with moss, grass and feathers around rim. Fork of tree.
CALL	Harsh 'churr' during flight.

RESIDENT/VISITOR
Mainly resident. Some winter on the Continent, while others migrate to British Isles from northern Europe in autumn.

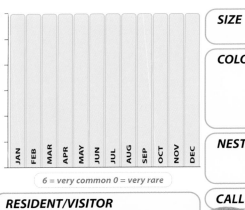

strong bill

whitish breast with dark spots

grey-brown back

powerful, long legs

♂

QUICK IDENTIFICATION

- **Large size compared to other thrushes**
- **Grey upperparts**
- **Dark, broad spots on breast**
- **White underwing visible in flight**

17

? ✓ Did it have a bold eyebrow marking?

? ✓ Was its beak short and thin?

? ✓ Were its flanks chestnut red in colour?

? ✓ Was it smaller than other thrushes?

I saw this bird on (date)

....

at (time)

....

It was (activity)

....

my notes

_____

_____

_____

_____

_____

my pictures

my observations

Redwing *(Turdus iliacus)*

Unlike the garden thrushes, the redwing is most commonly found in woods and fields in flocks, foraging for worms, slugs, snails, insects and berries. Sometimes it mixes with fieldfares and song thrushes. A flock of redwings will congregate on a berry tree and strip it bare before moving on. It breeds in open spruce and birch woods in northern Europe. It visits Britain in winter, and when freezing weather makes life difficult, it may visit the garden to feed from the bird-table, or forage through the flower borders. Flocks of migrating redwings can be identified at night by their piping calls.

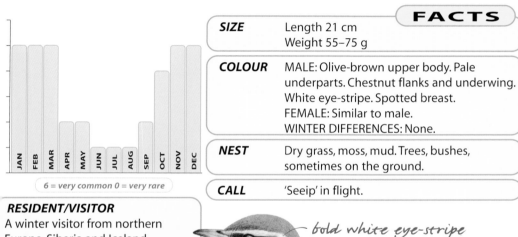

6 = very common 0 = very rare

FACTS

SIZE	Length 21 cm Weight 55–75 g
COLOUR	MALE: Olive-brown upper body. Pale underparts. Chestnut flanks and underwing. White eye-stripe. Spotted breast. FEMALE: Similar to male. WINTER DIFFERENCES: None.
NEST	Dry grass, moss, mud. Trees, bushes, sometimes on the ground.
CALL	'Seeip' in flight.

RESIDENT/VISITOR
A winter visitor from northern Europe, Siberia and Iceland. Some pairs have bred in northern Scotland.

bold white eye-stripe

whitish with speckles

👁 **QUICK IDENTIFICATION**

- **Moves and feeds in flocks**
- **Creamy white eye-stripe**
- **Chestnut underwing visible in flight**
- **Smaller than other thrushes**

♂ ♀

chestnut-red flanks

? ✓ Was its back chestnut brown?

? ✓ Was its tail black?

? ✓ Did it have a distinctive blue-grey head?

? ✓ Was it in a flock?

I saw this bird on (date)

....

at (time)

....

It was (activity)

....

my notes

my pictures

my observations

Fieldfare (*Turdus pilaris*)

This large and colourful thrush forages in noisy, chattering flocks in open fields and parks. As it feeds, the flock moves steadily forward across the ground. In cold winter weather it eagerly joins other birds at the bird-table. It also visits orchards to feed on rotten fruit still lying on the ground. Interestingly, whether feeding on the ground or roosting in a tree, the entire flock faces the same way. Fieldfares take off and wheel in flight all together, constantly calling. They roost together at night, usually on the ground, among shrubs and bushes, and even in the furrows of ploughed fields.

6 = very common 0 = very rare

RESIDENT/VISITOR
A winter visitor from Scandinavia and northern Europe.

FACTS

SIZE	Length 26 cm Weight 80–130 g
COLOUR	MALE: Blue-grey head and rump. Rusty brown back. Throat and breast, buff-yellow, with dark spots. White underbelly and underwings. Black tail. FEMALE: Similar to male. WINTER DIFFERENCES: None.
NEST	Untidy straw, grass, feathers. Usually in a hole in trees, buildings, cliffs, nest-boxes.
CALL	'Ee-eep' on ground. 'Chack – chack – chack' in flight.

👁 QUICK IDENTIFICATION

- **Contrasting colour scheme of grey and rust**
- **Beak has yellow base and dark tip**
- **White underwing in flight**
- **Flock behaviour, all facing same way**

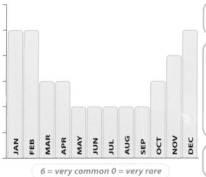

blue-grey head

chestnut-coloured back

speckled brown breast

dark tail

? ✓ **Was its bill bright orange-yellow?**

? ✓ **Were its feathers pure black?**

? ✓ **Was its song melodious?**

? ✓ **Was it feeding on the ground?**

I saw this bird on (date)

....

at (time)

....

It was (activity)

....

my notes

my pictures

my observations

Blackbird *(Turdus merula)*

The blackbird is a member of the thrush family. It is one of the most common garden birds and is found throughout Europe. Hopping and running along the ground, it scuffles noisily through dead leaves for worms, insects, fallen fruits and seeds. It is often seen tugging earthworms out of garden lawns, but stays close to leafy cover. The blackbird is an enthusiastic visitor to the bird-table. It is one of the earliest members of the dawn chorus, and likes to sit high on a tree or roof-top to sing its melodious, fluting song.

6 = very common 0 = very rare

FACTS

SIZE	Length 25 cm Weight 80–110 g
COLOUR	MALE: Coal-black plumage. Bright orange-yellow bill and eye-ring. FEMALE: Dark-brown back. Pale undersides. Mottled breast. WINTER DIFFERENCES: None.
NEST	Moss, grass, plastered with mud, lined with soft grass. Trees, hedges, wall-ivy. Not far from ground.
CALL	'Tchink, tchink' when uneasy or settling for the night. 'Tchook' when anxious. Loud cackling alarm.

RESIDENT/VISITOR
Resident, with some winter visitors from northern Europe.

👁 QUICK IDENTIFICATION

- **Loud alarm cackle**
- **Low, swooping flight**
- **Dipping tail when landing**
- **All-black male with bright yellow bill**

orange-yellow eye-ring

orange-yellow bill

pure black plumage in male

♂

? ✓ Did it have white cheeks?

? ✓ Was its tail pale blue and notched in shape?

? ✓ Was its belly yellow with a dark dividing line?

? ✓ Did it flit about?

I saw this bird on (date)

....

at (time)

....

It was (activity)

....

my notes

my pictures

my observations

Blue Tit *(Parus caeruleus)*

O ne of nature's great acrobats, the blue tit prefers oaks and birch trees in the wild, and has become one of the commonest garden birds. It is frequently seen at the bird-table, and repays its hosts by also feeding on garden pests such as greenfly. It readily hangs upside down to feed on lumps of fat or coconut halves suspended on a string. Sometimes it is known as the tomtit. The blue tit quickly becomes tame around humans and is notorious for stealing the cream from milk bottles after pecking through the foil top.

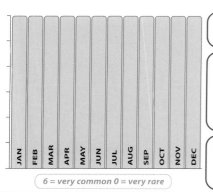

JAN FEB MAR APR MAY JUN JUL AUG SEP OCT NOV DEC

6 = very common 0 = very rare

RESIDENT/VISITOR
Resident.

FACTS

SIZE	Length 11.5 cm Weight 11 g
COLOUR	MALE: Blue crown, wings and tail. Head white at sides. Black stripe through eye. Yellow underparts. Greenish mantle. FEMALE: Paler colours than the male. WINTER DIFFERENCES: None.
NEST	Hair, wool or feathers on moss and dried grass. In holes, including trees, walls, banks, and even letter-boxes. Readily uses nest-boxes.
CALL	'Tsie-tsi-tsi'.

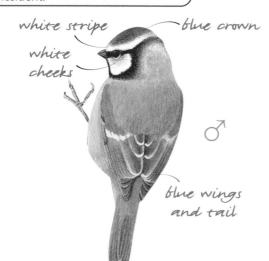

white stripe
blue crown
white cheeks
♂
blue wings and tail

👁 QUICK IDENTIFICATION

- **Blue cap, wings and tail**
- **Hangs and feeds from the slenderest twigs**
- **First occupant of nest-boxes in spring**
- **Fluttery flight and jerky movement**

? Was it small in size?

? Did it have two white wing bars?

? Was its voice high-pitched?

? Did it have a black bib?

I saw this bird on (date)

....

at (time)

....

It was (activity)

....

my notes

_____

_____

_____

_____

_____

my pictures

my observations

Coal Tit *(Parus ater)*

The coal tit is the smallest member of the tit family and is much shier than the blue tit. It occasionally uses a nest-box, and will visit the bird-table, but carries food away and hides it. The coal tit is naturally a bird of the forest. It forages in trees for live prey such as spiders and insects, and searches the ground for nuts and seeds. It has a preference for deep woods of conifers. An acrobatic bird, it can be seen creeping up tree trunks. It sometimes forages with mixed flocks of goldcrests and treecreepers through trees and bracken. The male sings its breeding calls from high in a tall tree.

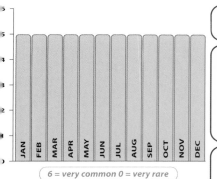

6 = very common 0 = very rare

RESIDENT/VISITOR
Resident.

FACTS

SIZE	Length 11.5 cm Weight 9 –11 g
COLOUR	MALE: Olive-brown upperparts. Buff underparts, paler on breast. White cheeks, with a black cap and throat. White nape. White wing bars. FEMALE: Similar to male. WINTER DIFFERENCES: None.
NEST	In hole, lined with moss, grass, hair or wool. Low in stump, wall, sometimes on ground.
CALL	'Tsui' or 'tsee'.

👁 QUICK IDENTIFICATION

- **Small size and dumpy, short-tailed shape**
- **White patch on nape**
- **Double white wing bars**
- **Feeds very high in tall pines**

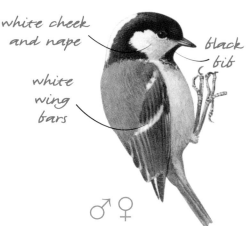

white cheek and nape

black bib

white wing bars

♂ ♀

? ✓ Was it bigger and bolder than other tits?

? ✓ Did it have white cheeks?

? ✓ Did it have a yellow bib and belly?

? ✓ Did it have a black, stubby bill?

I saw this bird on (date)

....

at (time)

....

It was (activity)

....

my notes

_____

_____

_____

_____

_____

_____

my pictures

my observations

Great Tit *(Parus major)*

The energetic great tit is one of the bullies of the bird-table, boisterously driving off shier birds as it muscles in on the free meal. It is the largest of the British tits, but is still extremely acrobatic. It will happily swing upside down to peck at a bone or suet ball on a string. Great tits have powerful beaks, and can be seen holding down nuts and other tough items with a foot to hammer away. They can even open hazelnuts with this technique. Despite appearing regularly in the garden, great tits are woodland birds. In winter they often forage in flocks over woodland floors, scratching for food.

JAN FEB MAR APR MAY JUN JUL AUG SEP OCT NOV DEC

6 = very common 0 = very rare

RESIDENT/VISITOR
Resident.

FACTS

SIZE	Length 14 cm Weight 19 g
COLOUR	MALE: Olive-green mantle, bright yellow underparts. Black cap circles white cheeks to join black throat, leading to wide black stripe to tail. Blue-grey rump, tail and wings. White wing bar and outer tail feathers. FEMALE: Breast stripe narrower than male's. Cap less glossy. WINTER DIFFERENCES: None.
NEST	Moss, lined with feathers and hair. In holes in trees, walls, hollow fence-posts.
CALL	Metallic 'ching'. Loud 'teacher – teacher' song.

👁 QUICK IDENTIFICATION

- **Large size, aggressive behaviour**
- **Black breast-to-tail stripe**
- **Black and yellow colour combination**
- **Metallic-sounding calls**

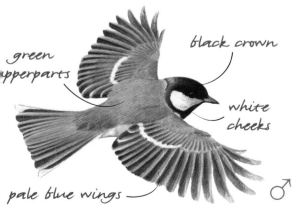

green upperparts

black crown

white cheeks

pale blue wings ♂

? ✓ Did it have a tail longer than its body?

? ✓ Were its underparts white and pink?

? ✓ Did it have a bold, black stripe over its eyes?

? ✓ Did it have a white crown?

I saw this bird on (date)

....

at (time)

....

It was (activity)

....

my notes

_____

_____

_____

_____

_____

my pictures

Long-tailed Tit *(Aegithalos caudatus)*

Apart from its long tail, this is one of our tiniest birds. It is not a true member of the tit family, and usually moves in small flocks seeking insects for food. Because of its small size, it is vulnerable to cold, and flock members huddle together to keep warm at night. Parents also cram themselves into the nest with up to a dozen young. The long-tailed tit was almost exterminated by severe frosts in 1947 in Britain. It uses its tiny beak to harvest insects, and also feeds on buds, and small amounts of lichen and algae in the trees.

JAN FEB MAR APR MAY JUN JUL AUG SEP OCT NOV DEC

6 = very common 0 = very rare

RESIDENT/VISITOR
Resident.

FACTS

SIZE	Length 14 cm Weight 8 g
COLOUR	MALE: Dull white throat and head, with black stripes over the eye, leading to black on upper neck and back. Rosy shoulder patches, lower back and underparts. Black wings and tail. Partly white outer tail feathers. FEMALE: Same as male. WINTER DIFFERENCES: None.
NEST	An oval of moss, wool, spiders' webs and lichen, lined with thousands of feathers. Side entry hole. Built in thick hedges, holly bushes, ivy-clad trees.
CALL	'Zee – zee' and 'trrr'.

👁 QUICK IDENTIFICATION

- **Long tail, small, round body**
- **Fluffy pink and white plumage**
- **Communal huddling at night**
- **Broad black line over eye**

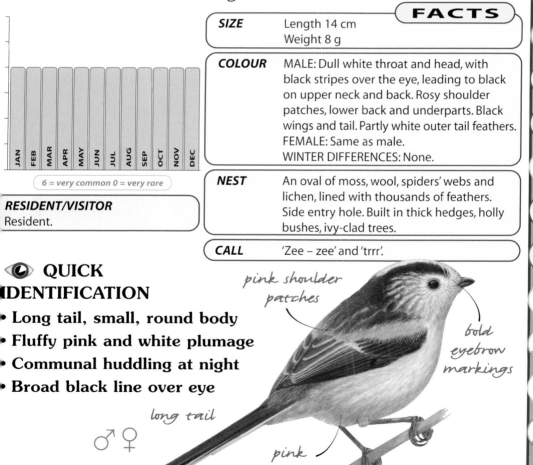

pink shoulder patches

bold eyebrow markings

long tail

♂♀

pink underparts

? ✓ Did it have a short, stubby bill?

? ✓ Was its cap glossy black?

? ✓ Was it an elegant looking little bird?

? ✓ Was its flight flitting and wavy?

I saw this bird on (date)

....

at (time)

....

It was (activity)

....

my notes

_____

_____

_____

_____

_____

my pictures

my observations

Marsh Tit *(Parus palustris)*

The marsh tit has been misnamed, for it does not frequent marshes. It prefers woodlands, where it hunts through the trees for insects, and forages on the ground for seeds. It holds tough seeds, such as beechmast, with one foot while it pecks them open with its strong beak. The marsh tit often teams up with roving flocks of several tit species, and it appears in gardens in the winter if food is put out. It does not linger at the bird-table, but carries food away to eat later, and hides it either in the ground, or in cracks in tree bark.

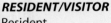

JAN FEB MAR APR MAY JUN JUL AUG SEP OCT NOV DEC

6 = very common 0 = very rare

RESIDENT/VISITOR
Resident.

FACTS

SIZE	Length 11.5 cm Weight 11 g
COLOUR	MALE: Glossy black cap extending down nape, and a neat black chin patch. Grey-white cheeks, neck sides, underparts. Grey-brown back. FEMALE: Same as male. WINTER DIFFERENCES: None.
NEST	Pad of hair and moss inside a natural hole in a tree. Sometimes in a wall. Rarely in a nest-box.
CALL	Shrill 'pitchu'. Song – 'chip, chip, chip'.

short bill

glossy black cap

small, black bib

♂ ♀

👁 **QUICK IDENTIFICATION**

- **Glossy black cap**
- **Regular ground feeder (unlike very similar willow tit)**
- **Distinctive sneeze-like 'pitchu' call**
- **Smaller head than willow tit**

? ✓ Was it tiny?

? ✓ Was its face plain with moustache streak?

? ✓ Was its body round?

? ✓ Did it have a golden-orange breast?

I saw this bird on (date)

....

at (time)

....

It was (activity)

....

my notes

_____

_____

_____

_____

_____

my pictures

my observations

Goldcrest (Regulus regulus)

Europe's smallest bird, the goldcrest still manages to migrate across the North Sea from Scandinavia to spend the winter in Britain. Like other tiny birds, it is very vulnerable to severe weather, but always seems to bounce back after cold seasons which almost wipe it out. True to its name, the male goldcrest raises his bright crest when courting, and also when rivals stray into his territory. Goldcrests mingle with tits and firecrests, which are closely related, in food-hunting winter flocks. Their main food consists of spiders and small insects such as aphids. Goldcrests are found in woodland, and in parks and gardens containing conifers like larch and fir.

JAN FEB MAR APR MAY JUN JUL AUG SEP OCT NOV DEC

6 = very common 0 = very rare

RESIDENT/VISITOR
A partial migrant. Some resident all year round. Others visit for the winter from Scandinavia.

FACTS

SIZE	Length 9 cm Weight 5–7 g
COLOUR	MALE: Dull green upperparts, creamy buff underparts. White bar and black patch on wing. Bright orange crest with black surround. FEMALE: Similar to male, but with paler, lemony crest. WINTER DIFFERENCES: None.
NEST	Basket-shaped nest woven from lichens, moss and spiders' webs, suspended under conifer branch.
CALL	High-pitched 'zeek' and trill. Also 'si-si-si'.

👁 QUICK IDENTIFICATION

- **Tiny and aggressive, flarable crest**
- **Large black eye for its size**
- **Can hover while hunting insects**
- **Thin, high voice**

fine moustache streak

distinctive golden-orange crest

round body   ♂

? ✓ Did it have a white eyebrow?

? ✓ Was its bill long and curved?

? ✓ Was it well camouflaged?

? ✓ Was its tail pointed?

my notes

I saw this bird on (date)

....

at (time)

....

It was (activity)

....

my pictures

my observations

Treecreeper *(Certhia familiaris)*

The treecreeper is an inconspicuous little bird, but is easily recognized by its long, curving beak, which it uses to probe bark as it creeps up the tree trunk. Almost always working upwards from the bottom of the trunk, the treecreeper uses its stiff tail feathers as a support against the bark. As it creeps upwards it spirals around the tree trunk, then flies down to the bottom of the next tree. The treecreeper occasionally comes into gardens, but will not usually approach the bird-table. It can be fed in the garden by smearing fat onto a tree trunk.

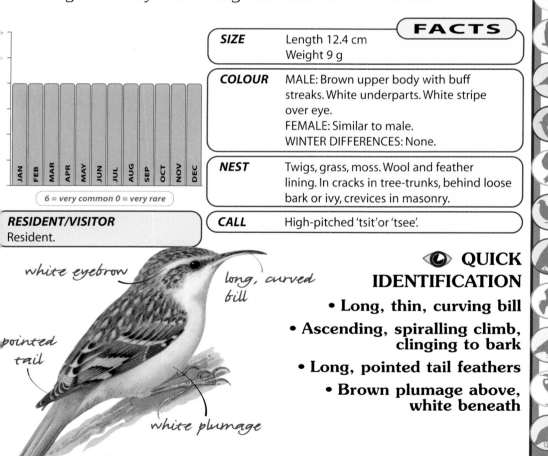

JAN FEB MAR APR MAY JUN JUL AUG SEP OCT NOV DEC

6 = very common 0 = very rare

RESIDENT/VISITOR
Resident.

white eyebrow

long, curved bill

pointed tail

white plumage

♂ ♀

FACTS

SIZE	Length 12.4 cm Weight 9 g
COLOUR	MALE: Brown upper body with buff streaks. White underparts. White stripe over eye. FEMALE: Similar to male. WINTER DIFFERENCES: None.
NEST	Twigs, grass, moss. Wool and feather lining. In cracks in tree-trunks, behind loose bark or ivy, crevices in masonry.
CALL	High-pitched 'tsit' or 'tsee'.

👁 QUICK IDENTIFICATION

- **Long, thin, curving bill**
- **Ascending, spiralling climb, clinging to bark**
- **Long, pointed tail feathers**
- **Brown plumage above, white beneath**

37

? ✓ Did it have a bright orange breast?

? ✓ Was it similar to a chaffinch?

? ✓ Were its legs red?

? ✓ Was its belly white?

I saw this bird on (date)

....

at (time)

....

It was (activity)

....

my notes

_____

_____

_____

_____

_____

my pictures

my observations

Brambling *(Fringilla montifringilla)*

The brambling is related to the chaffinch. It is very fond of beech woods, foraging through them in flocks sometimes numbering thousands. When they have eaten all the available food in one place, the flock decamps to find a new supply. When beech-mast crops fail, or when the weather is particularly harsh, the brambling is attracted to gardens where food has been put out. It is basically a ground feeder, and usually takes the seeds and other scraps dropped from the table by other birds. Bramblings often move in mixed flocks containing chaffinches and other finches as they hunt for insects and seeds on the woodland floor.

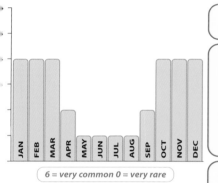

6 = very common 0 = very rare

FACTS

SIZE	Length 14.5 cm Weight 25 g
COLOUR	MALE: Orange breast and shoulders. Black head and back. White rump, with white bands on wings. Red legs. FEMALE: Duller, with brown head and back, and yellowish breast and shoulders. WINTER DIFFERENCES: Male orange and black feathers duller due to brown tips.
NEST	Moss, plant stalks and lichen. In trees, including conifers.
CALL	'Kvek' when flying. Single 'dzwee' song.

RESIDENT/VISITOR
Winter visitor arriving from Scandinavia in autumn, returning in spring.

black head and back with scaling in winter

bright orange plumage

white belly

👁 QUICK IDENTIFICATION

White rump visible in flight

Black head of male in spring

Orange breast and shoulder patch

Habit of flocking in beech woods

? Was it seen singly or in a pair? ✓

? Did it have a bright pink breast? ✓

? Was its crown black? ✓

? Was it a thickset bird? ✓

I saw this bird on (date)

....

at (time)

....

It was (activity)

....

my notes

_____

_____

_____

_____

_____

my pictures

Bullfinch *(Pyrrhula pyrrhula)*

Bullfinches are often seen in couples, and are thought to pair for life. They are shy and secretive birds, and like to stay close to cover. The bullfinch rarely forages on the ground, and is usually spotted in trees and bushes, using its strong beak to harvest seeds, berries and buds. Its fondness for buds when other food is scarce has made it a very unpopular bird with fruit farmers, as a pair of hungry bullfinches can do severe damage to the growing points of a fruit tree in the spring. In autumn and early winter the bullfinch feeds on seeds such as ash keys. Rare at the bird-table, it will take shelled peanuts from a net.

6 = very common 0 = very rare

RESIDENT/VISITOR
Resident.

FACTS

SIZE	Length 15 cm Weight 21–27 g
COLOUR	MALE: Smoke-grey upperparts. Rosy red underparts. Black forehead, crown, chin and bill. Black on wings and tail. White wing bars and under base of tail. FEMALE: Pale brown upperparts. Pinkish underparts. Hind-neck grey. Black and white as male. WINTER DIFFERENCES: None.
NEST	Twig foundation. Lined with rootlets and hair. Low and concealed.
CALL	Distinct, low, piping 'phew'.

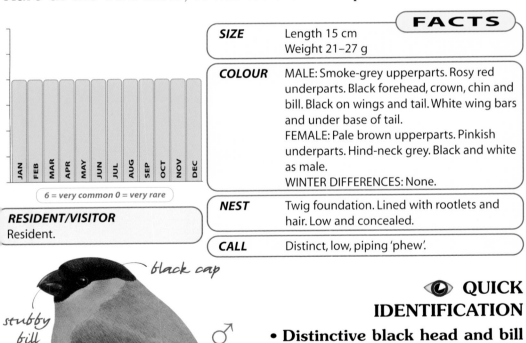

black cap

stubby bill

♂

rosy-red breast

white rump

QUICK IDENTIFICATION

- **Distinctive black head and bill**
- **White rump flash in flight**
- **Unusual rosy red breast of male**
- **Puffed feathers, swaying mating display**

41

? ✓ Was its breast and throat pinkish in colour?

? ✓ Was its bill blue-grey and stubby?

? ✓ Was its tail a notched shape?

? ✓ Did it have a blue-grey head?

I saw this bird on (date)

....

at (time)

....

It was (activity)

....

my notes

my pictures

my observations

Chaffinch (*Fringilla coelebs*)

The chaffinch is one of Britain's most common and popular garden birds. It rarely strays over a 5 kilometre radius of its nest. It is found everywhere, from open commons and gardens to woods and farmland. A very bold visitor to the bird-table, it enthusiastically consumes scraps, seeds and berries, and soon becomes quite tame. The chaffinch is sociable and roosts in groups in hedges. It forages in the winter in the company of bramblings, greenfinches, yellowhammers and sparrows. The female is the main nest-builder, though the male brings some of the materials. She does most of the hatching, but both parents feed the young.

JAN	FEB	MAR	APR	MAY	JUN	JUL	AUG	SEP	OCT	NOV	DEC

6 = very common 0 = very rare

RESIDENT/VISITOR
Resident, with many winter visitors from Europe.

FACTS

SIZE	Length 15 cm Weight 19–23 g
COLOUR	MALE: Grey head. Chestnut back. Pink-brown face and breast. White wing bars and outer tail feathers. Olive-green rump. FEMALE: Olive-brown head and back. Pale pink breast. WINTER DIFFERENCES: None.
NEST	Carefully woven from moss, grass, roots, camouflaged with lichens and spiders' webs. Tree fork, hedgerow or thick bush.
CALL	'Chwink' repeated. 'Choop' in flight.

 QUICK IDENTIFICATION

- **Grey cap of male with pink-brown face and breast**
- **Double white wing bars in flight**
- **'Choop' flight call in winter flocks**
- **Olive-green rump in flight**

grey cap

chestnut back

pink breast

notch-shaped tail

♂

? Did it have a crimson-red face?

? Was there a yellow patch on its wing?

? Did it have a tinkling voice?

? Was its beak short and stubby?

I saw this bird on (date)

....

at (time)

....

It was (activity)

....

my notes

_____

_____

_____

_____

_____

my pictures

Goldfinch (Carduelis carduelis)

The goldfinch stands out amongst other garden birds for the sheer brilliance and contrasts of its colouring. It is sometimes known as the 'thistle finch', because it has a great fondness for certain plants such as thistles, dandelions and teazels. It flutters around their seed-heads, delicately extracting the seeds with its sharply pointed beak. The goldfinch rarely comes to the bird-table, but may be tempted by seeds and strings of peanuts. In the autumn it sometimes teams up with redpolls and siskins to forage for seeds. It also eats small insects. Its feeding grounds include gardens, wastelands, orchards and roadsides.

JAN	FEB	MAR	APR	MAY	JUN	JUL	AUG	SEP	OCT	NOV	DEC

6 = very common 0 = very rare

RESIDENT/VISITOR
Resident.

FACTS

SIZE	Length 12 cm Weight 14–17 g
COLOUR	MALE: Cap black. Cheeks, throat, underparts white. Brilliant red face. Black tail and wings. Bright yellow wing band. Brown mantle. FEMALE: Similar, with less red on face. WINTER DIFFERENCES: None.
NEST	Roots, grass, moss, lichen, lined with plant down or wool. Placed right at end of tree branch, or in dense hedge.
CALL	'Swit-wit-wit' perched or in flight.

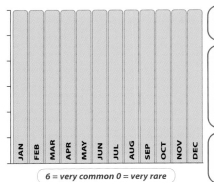

stubby bill

bright yellow and black wing

crimson red face

♂

👁 QUICK IDENTIFICATION

- **Bright contrasting black, white and red on head**
- **Broad yellow wing bar in flight**
- **Fluttering flight round seed heads**
- **Prefers down-producing plants**

45

Was it a chunky-looking bird? Yes

Did it have a thick bill?

Was its upper plumage olive-green?

Were its underparts yellow?

I saw this bird on (date)
13.3.12

at (time)
08:15

It was (activity)
Waiting for feed

my notes

my pictures

my observations

Greenfinch *(Carduelis chloris)*

The greenfinch is a common garden visitor, and is particularly keen on sunflower seeds and peanuts. It likes to feed in company with others, and moves in groups in trees and on the ground. The greenfinch is a chunky bird, with a strong bill which it uses on tough seeds. It has a varied diet which includes berries and buds, as well as insects such as ants and aphids. It can become quite aggressive if there is competition for food, and often drives other birds away from favourite food sources such as peanut feeders. It enjoys garden berries such as cotoneaster and yew.

JAN FEB MAR APR MAY JUN JUL AUG SEP OCT NOV DEC

6 = very common 0 = very rare

RESIDENT/VISITOR
Resident. Some visiting migrants come from Europe in autumn, departing again in spring.

FACTS

SIZE	Length 14.5 cm Weight 25–31 g
COLOUR	MALE: Olive-green upper plumage, with a lighter, more yellow rump. Brighter yellow in tail and wings. Upper wing surfaces grey-green. FEMALE: Duller, with less yellow showing. WINTER DIFFERENCES: Brown tips to green plumage in winter.
NEST	Woven twigs and moss, lined with roots, hair and feathers. In hedgerows and evergreen bushes.
CALL	Drawn-out 'tswee'.

QUICK IDENTIFICATION

- **Yellow in tail and wings visible in flight**
- **Aggressive at the bird-table**
- **Large, swirling, feeding flocks**
- **Bat-like, circling mating flight**

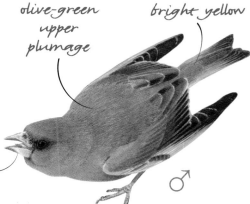

olive-green upper plumage

bright yellow

thick bill

♂

? ✓ Were its upperparts bright yellow?

? ✓ Did it have a black cap?

? ✓ Did it have a V-notch tail?

? ✓ Did it have streaked flanks?

I saw this bird on (date)

....

at (time)

....

It was (activity)

....

my notes

my pictures

my observations

Siskin (Carduelis spinus)

The siskin likes to live in coniferous woods but will nest in pine trees in the garden. At one time resident siskins lived mostly in Scotland and Ireland, though now the species has spread further south in Britain due to an increase in conifer plantations. The siskin is mainly a seed-eater, and clings to twigs in a tit-like manner as it extracts them. In the garden it heads for the peanuts, especially those in red plastic nets, which it perhaps mistakes for pine cones. In winter the siskin goes foraging in company with redpolls through the top branches of spruce, birch, larch and alder trees.

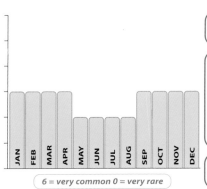

JAN FEB MAR APR MAY JUN JUL AUG SEP OCT NOV DEC

6 = very common 0 = very rare

RESIDENT/VISITOR
Mainly a winter visitor from Scandinavia and the Baltic, but resident populations are increasing.

FACTS

SIZE	Length 12 cm Weight 12–18 g
COLOUR	MALE: Yellow-green upperparts, paler beneath. Yellow rump, wing bar, eye-stripe, sides of tail. Brown-streaked back and flanks. Black crown and chin. FEMALE: Duller. Less yellow. No black on head. WINTER DIFFERENCES: None.
NEST	Twigs and moss. Usually at end of conifer branch.
CALL	Squeaky 'tzy-zi'. Wheezy 'tsewi' in flight.

👁 QUICK IDENTIFICATION

- **Bright yellow wing bars**
- **Smaller and slimmer than greenfinch**
- **Distinct V-notch in tail visible in flight**
- **Tit-like feeding behaviour**

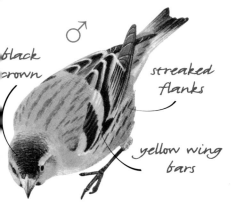

♂

black crown

streaked flanks

yellow wing bars

49

? ✓ Did it have a black bib?

? ✓ Were its upperparts brown and black streaked?

? ✓ Did it twitter?

? ✓ Did it have a grey crown?

I saw this bird on (date)

....

at (time)

....

It was (activity)

....

my notes

_____

_____

_____

_____

_____

my pictures

my observations

House Sparrow (*Passer domesticus*)

The house sparrow is the street urchin of the bird world and goes around in noisy gangs looking for food. It turns up everywhere – gardens, wasteland, farms, railways – wherever the chance of food arises. It feeds on wild seeds, spilled grain, insects, scraps – anything. In winter it finds both food and warmth in farm stock-pens and stables. It can crowd out other birds at feeding-sites, though its numbers have fallen in recent years. It has learned useful bird-table techniques such as hovering, and hanging upside down to get at food in suspended feeders. The house sparrow is a successful survivor which has spread throughout the world.

JAN FEB MAR APR MAY JUN JUL AUG SEP OCT NOV DEC

6 = very common 0 = very rare

RESIDENT/VISITOR
Resident.

FACTS

SIZE	Length 14.5 cm Weight 22–31 g
COLOUR	MALE: Grey crown. Red-brown border and nape. Pale grey cheeks merging into breast and underparts. Black around eye and into throat. Wings warm brown with black markings. FEMALE: Duller. Paler back. No facial black. Pale eye band. WINTER DIFFERENCES: Male loses sharp colour contrast due to temporary pale feather tips.
NEST	Untidy – straw, grass, lined with feathers. In holes and crevices in buildings. Also in trees and hedgerows. Often in colonies.
CALL	Loud 'cheep'. Constant twittering.

👁 QUICK IDENTIFICATION

- **Grey crown on male**
- **Strong contrast between male and female**
- **White wing bar in flight**
- **Quarrelsome groups always on the move**

grey crown

brown and black streaked back

large, dark bib

♂

? ☑ Did it have a white moustache?

? ☑ Was its collar white?

? ☑ Was its head black?

? ☑ Did it fly in a short, jerky way?

I saw this bird on (date)

....

at (time)

....

It was (activity)

....

my notes

my pictures

my observations

Reed Bunting (*Emberiza schoeniclus*)

True to its name, the reed bunting is a bird of the wetlands. It has, however, now spread into some drier habitats. In the winter it leaves its reed-beds, marshes and upland areas, and moves to the fields. Here it hunts for seeds and insects alongside finches, and other buntings, like the yellowhammer. If threatened by approaching danger, the reed bunting pretends to be injured, crawling along with wings half-spread, leading the threat away from its nest. Because it is primarily a ground feeder, it is in danger of starvation when there is snow cover, and increasingly visits gardens in the winter for food.

JAN FEB MAR APR MAY JUN JUL AUG SEP OCT NOV DEC

6 = very common 0 = very rare

RESIDENT/VISITOR
Resident, but many continental reed buntings winter in Britain.

FACTS	
SIZE	Length 15.5 cm Weight 19 g
COLOUR	MALE: Black head and throat. White collar, underparts and moustache. Chestnut back and wings with dark markings. Brown and grey tail with white outer feathers. FEMALE: Brown head. Pale eyebrow and moustache. Buff underparts. Back and wings ruddier than male. WINTER DIFFERENCES: Head and throat grey-brown.
NEST	Leaves, grass, moss, hair lining. On vegetation in marshy ground.
CALL	Loud 'tseek', and metallic 'chink'.

white collar

black head

white moustache

white breast

♂

QUICK IDENTIFICATION

- **Male's black head and white moustache**
- **Long-tailed, wave-like flight**
- **Sings from reed-stem perch**
- **Often feeds in mixed bunting groups**

? ✓ Did it have a sharp, rather tuneless call?

? ✓ Were its head, throat and breast grey?

? ✓ Were its upperparts dark-streaked and its back brown?

? ✓ Was its beak thin?

I saw this bird on (date)

....

at (time)

....

It was (activity)

....

my notes

_____

_____

_____

_____

_____

my pictures

my observations

Dunnock *(Prunella modularis)*

Also known, incorrectly, as the hedge sparrow, the dunnock is not related to sparrows. It is a quiet and furtive bird, and creeps, mouse-like, along hedges and under bushes as it seeks the caterpillars, spiders and insects on which it feeds. In winter the dunnock is attracted to the garden bird-table, but it is more hesitant than many other birds. It also carries out insect searches in crop fields, copses and along roadsides. The dunnock is found all over the British Isles except for the most northerly Scottish islands. It is often chosen as an unwitting foster parent by cuckoos.

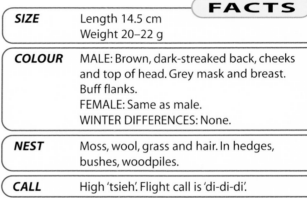

JAN FEB MAR APR MAY JUN JUL AUG SEP OCT NOV DEC

6 = very common 0 = very rare

FACTS

SIZE	Length 14.5 cm Weight 20–22 g
COLOUR	MALE: Brown, dark-streaked back, cheeks and top of head. Grey mask and breast. Buff flanks. FEMALE: Same as male. WINTER DIFFERENCES: None.
NEST	Moss, wool, grass and hair. In hedges, bushes, woodpiles.
CALL	High 'tsieh'. Flight call is 'di-di-di'.

RESIDENT/VISITOR
Mainly resident, though some birds move southwards in autumn, and some even cross the Channel.

QUICK IDENTIFICATION

• Unlike sparrows, has thin beak of insect-eater

• Hops slowly, hunched close to ground

• Often in a trio – two males, one female

• Several birds may perform wing-waving display together

grey eye-stripe, throat and breast

thin, sharp beak

♂♀

? ✓ Did it have a crimson-red crown?

? ✓ Did it have a yellow rump?

? ✓ Was its moustache red and black?

? ✓ Was its call loud and like laughter?

I saw this bird on (date)

at (time)

It was (activity)

my notes

my pictures

my observations

Green Woodpecker *(Picus viridis)*

The handsome green woodpecker lives in woodlands and parklands, and is Britain's largest woodpecker. It is a shy but noisy bird, and is unmistakable, especially in flight, with its bold colouring. Also unmistakable is its raucous 'yaffle' – a loud cry resembling hysterical laughter. The green woodpecker uses its long, pointed beak to excavate its nest-hole and to dig for ants, its main food. The ants stick to the woodpecker's long, sticky tongue. In the garden it is more likely to drill the lawn for ants than approach the bird-table. When ants' nests are frozen hard, it has been known to bore into beehives.

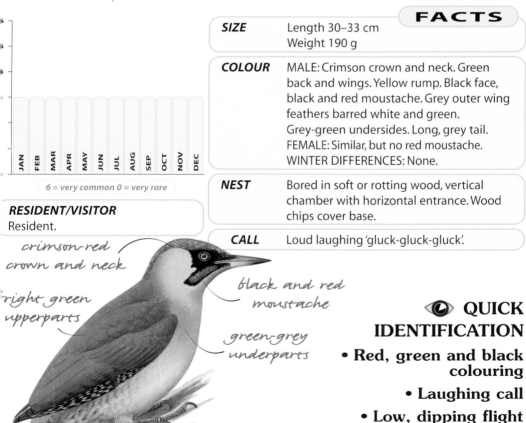

JAN FEB MAR APR MAY JUN JUL AUG SEP OCT NOV DEC

6 = very common 0 = very rare

RESIDENT/VISITOR
Resident.

crimson-red crown and neck

bright green upperparts

black and red moustache

green-grey underparts

♂

FACTS

SIZE	Length 30–33 cm Weight 190 g
COLOUR	MALE: Crimson crown and neck. Green back and wings. Yellow rump. Black face, black and red moustache. Grey outer wing feathers barred white and green. Grey-green undersides. Long, grey tail. FEMALE: Similar, but no red moustache. WINTER DIFFERENCES: None.
NEST	Bored in soft or rotting wood, vertical chamber with horizontal entrance. Wood chips cover base.
CALL	Loud laughing 'gluck-gluck-gluck'.

QUICK IDENTIFICATION

• **Red, green and black colouring**
• **Laughing call**
• **Low, dipping flight**
• **Pointed beak, long tail feathers**

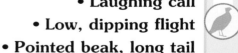

? ✓ **Did it have a black crown?**

? ✓ **Was the nape of its neck red?**

? ✓ **Were there bold white markings on its black back?**

? ✓ **Were its undertail feathers bright red?**

I saw this bird on (date)

....

at (time)

....

It was (activity)

....

my notes

....
....
....
....

my pictures

my observations

Great Spotted Woodpecker *(Dendrocopus major)*

The most common woodpecker in Britain, the great spotted woodpecker is more likely to be seen in gardens than the green woodpecker, and is very partial to fat and peanuts. Unfortunately, it is also known to take young birds, such as blue tits, out of nest-boxes. The great spotted woodpecker gets most of its food by pecking at bark and rotten wood to extract insects and their larvae. It has also been seen wedging nuts into bark crevices, then cracking them with its beak. It defines its territory by 'drumming' – striking a branch with its bill in short bursts of rapid blows, a sound which can be heard over long distances.

6 = very common 0 = very rare

JAN FEB MAR APR MAY JUN JUL AUG SEP OCT NOV DEC

RESIDENT/VISITOR
Resident.

FACTS

SIZE	Length 22–23 cm Weight 80 g
COLOUR	MALE: Black cap and collar. Crimson nape. White cheeks. Black back and wings with white patches and white barred primary feathers. Crimson undertail. FEMALE: No red nape. WINTER DIFFERENCES: None.
NEST	Cavity freshly dug out each year, usually in a dead tree or stump.
CALL	'Tchik' repeated.

👁 QUICK IDENTIFICATION

- **White wing patches and red undertail in flight**
- **Loud 'tchik' call**
- **Upright posture perched on vertical surface**
- **Distinctive territorial drumming**

red nape of neck

red undertail

white wing patches

♂

? ✓ Was the bird very small, almost sparrow-size?

? ✓ Was it mainly black and white coloured?

? ✓ Was the crown bright red?

? ✓ Was it an agile climber?

I saw this bird on (date)

....

at (time)

....

It was (activity)

....

my notes

....

....

....

....

....

my pictures

my observations

Lesser Spotted Woodpecker *(Dendrocopus minor)*

The lesser spotted woodpecker is about the size of a sparrow. Its colouring is like the greater spotted woodpecker's but arranged differently. It is a shy bird hunting insects out of sight in high branches. It drums to mark its territory. Unlike other woodpeckers, it joins winter feeding flocks of mixed tits. It is hardly ever seen at the bird-table, approaching it very nervously if at all. It is normally only seen in England and Wales.

6 = very common   0 = very rare

RESIDENT/VISITOR
Resident.

FACTS

SIZE	Length 13–14 cm Weight 20 g
COLOUR	MALE: Red crown. Black nape, moustache stripes, throat, back and tail. White face, brownish white underparts, broad white wing bars. FEMALE: Less bright, and with whitish crown. WINTER DIFFERENCES: None.
NEST	Excavated by both birds in rotten wood up to 25 m above the ground. Very small entry hole – 3 cm wide.
CALL	'Kee-kee-kee'. Weak 'tchik'.

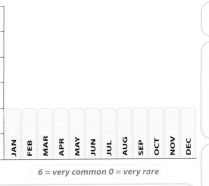

black and white feathers

red colour

short, grey, thin bill

♂

👁 QUICK IDENTIFICATION

- **Bright red crown of male**
- **Bold white wing bars**
- **Fluttering to remain in position when feeding**
- **Woodpecker shape, tiny size**

61

? ☑ Did it have a large rounded head?

? ☑ Did it have a distinctive facial disc?

? ☑ Was its tail short and square?

? ☑ Was its bill hooked?

I saw this bird on (date)

....

at (time)

....

It was (activity)

....

my notes

my observations

Tawny Owl (*Strix aluco*)

This woodland predator is now also found in parks and gardens. Where once it hunted small mammals for its food, it has switched in urban areas to hunting small birds. Any appearance at the bird-table is in pursuit of fellow guests! It uses a different perch at night, usually high up, and from here it calls to contact mates and warn off rivals. It flies in eery silence, its wing-beats muffled by downy edges on its wing feathers. As well as mammals and birds, the tawny owl also feeds on insects, frogs and newts. In city habitats it sometimes catches bats such as pipistrelles and noctules.

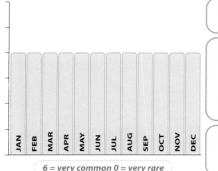

6 = very common 0 = very rare

RESIDENT/VISITOR
Resident.

FACTS

SIZE	Length 37–39 cm Weight 350–500 g
COLOUR	MALE: Red-brown to grey upperparts. Buff underparts, with distinct, dark streaking. Grey-brown facial discs. Black eyes. FEMALE: Same as male. WINTER DIFFERENCES: None.
NEST	Hole in tree. Also uses old crow and heron nests, squirrel dreys, holes in farm buildings. No nesting material used.
CALL	'Kewick'. Song – 'hoo hoooo'.

👁 QUICK IDENTIFICATION

- Familiar hooting song
- Black eyes in grey-brown facial discs
- Large size, no ear tufts
- Clearly seen at evening on hunting perch

distinctive facial disc and dark eyes

mottled brown feathers

♂ ♀

? Were its upperparts light brown?

? Did it have a warbling voice?

? Were its underparts buffy coloured?

? Was its bill short and thickish?

I saw this bird on (date)

....

at (time)

....

It was (activity)

....

my notes

my pictures

my observations

Garden Warbler *(Sylvia borin)*

The garden warbler is a summer visitor which could be easily overlooked with its bland, mousy colouring. But it has a glorious singing voice. Despite its name, it is rarely seen in any but the largest gardens, as it prefers to live in overgrown hedges, woodlands with thick undergrowth, and bushy commons. Related to the black cap, and sharing its migration pattern, the garden warbler avoids competition with its relative by feeding at a lower level. It is an insect-eater, but also feeds on berries and fruit when insects become scarce in late autumn.

JAN FEB MAR APR MAY JUN JUL AUG SEP OCT NOV DEC

6 = very common 0 = very rare

RESIDENT/VISITOR
Summer visitor, arriving in April and returning to sub-Saharan Africa in late October.

FACTS

SIZE	Length 13–15 cm Weight 16–23 g
COLOUR	MALE: Light brown upperparts. Paler buff underparts. Pale, narrow eye-ring. Faint, grey neck spot. FEMALE: Same as male. WINTER DIFFERENCES: None.
NEST	Cup-shaped, made of dry grass, and lined with rootlets and hair. Low in bushes, including rhododendrons, and brambles.
CALL	'Check – check'. Warbling, bubbling song with long phrases and pure tones.

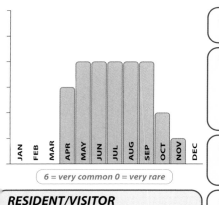

pale, narrow eye-ring

light brown plumage

short, thickish bill

buffy underparts

👁 QUICK IDENTIFICATION

- Short, square-ended tail visible in flight
- Smooth colouring lacking sharp contrasts
- Sustained warbling song with long phrases
- Compact, stocky build

? ☑ Did it look like a chiffchaff?

? ☑ Did it have a yellow eye-stripe?

? ☑ Were its legs pale?

? ☑ Did it have a notch-shaped tail?

I saw this bird on (date)

....

at (time)

....

It was (activity)

....

my notes

_____

_____

_____

_____

_____

my pictures

Willow Warbler *(Phylloscopus trochilus)*

Flying in from North Africa every spring, the willow warbler is one of the most commonly seen summer visitors to Europe. On its arrival in Britain it often refuels by feeding on insects found on flowering willows. The willow warbler is full of nervous energy, and is forever on the move, flicking its wings as it busily forages for insects. A fine singer, it sings its song from trees and bushes, while working its way through foliage seeking insects, and while flying. When courting the female, the male perches near her and slowly waves one or both of his wings at her.

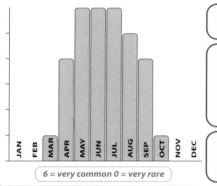

6 = very common 0 = very rare

RESIDENT/VISITOR
A summer visitor from North Africa, arriving in Britain in April, and returning there in September.

FACTS

SIZE	Length 11 cm Weight 6–10 g
COLOUR	MALE: Olive-brown upperparts. Yellow breast. Whitish underparts. Yellow stripe over eye. Wing and tail feathers dusky. FEMALE: Same as male. WINTER DIFFERENCES: None.
NEST	Half-dome shape, made of grass and lined with feathers. On the ground, beneath furze bushes, in hedge banks.
CALL	'Hoo-id' – two syllables. Song – a falling sequence of clear notes.

👁 QUICK IDENTIFICATION

- Yellowish tones to plumage
- Yellow stripe over eye
- Sometimes flutters like a fly-catcher when hunting
- Cascading, liquid song

yellow eye-stripe

olive-brown plumage

pale legs

♂ ♀

? ✓ Was it rather like a willow warbler?

? ✓ Was its voice a distinctive chiffchaff call?

? ✓ Did it have a cream line above the eye and eye-ring?

? ✓ Were its legs dark-coloured?

I saw this bird on (date)

....

at (time)

....

It was (activity)

....

my notes

_____

_____

_____

_____

_____

my pictures

Chiffchaff *(Phylloscopus collybita)*

The chiffchaff is sometimes known as the 'leaf warbler' because of its excellent colour camouflage in foliage. It feeds mainly high up in trees, on caterpillars and tiny insects such as midges. The male arrives in this country before the female and lays claim to nesting territory with loud singing. The hen hatches the young and looks after them with little or no help from the male. Chiffchaffs are occasionally seen at the bird-table, but they are likely to be from the minority which overwinter here. It is possible that bird-table food supplies have influenced the increase in visitors such as the chiffchaff, which have begun to stay all year round.

JAN FEB MAR APR MAY JUN JUL AUG SEP OCT NOV DEC

6 = very common 0 = very rare

RESIDENT/VISITOR
Visitor from around the Mediterranean. One of first visiting songbirds to arrive in March. Some have become residents.

FACTS

SIZE	Length 11 cm Weight 6–9 g
COLOUR	MALE: Brownish olive head and back. Grey-white underparts. Pale yellow breast. Cream line above eye and eye-ring. FEMALE: Same as male. WINTER DIFFERENCES: None.
NEST	Dry grass, moss, leaves, feathers. On or near ground. Domed.
CALL	'Hweet'. Song – 'chiff-chaff' and variations, repeated.

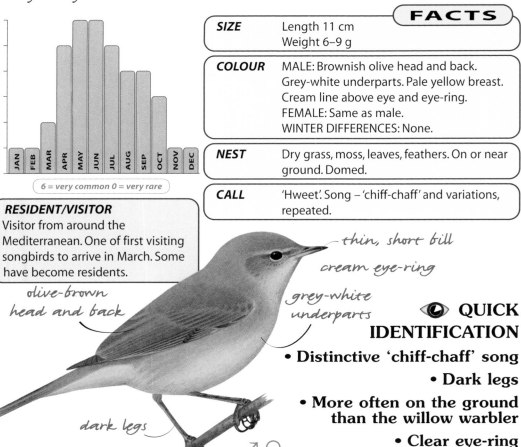

thin, short bill

cream eye-ring

grey-white underparts

olive-brown head and back

dark legs

♂ ♀

QUICK IDENTIFICATION

- **Distinctive 'chiff-chaff' song**
- **Dark legs**
- **More often on the ground than the willow warbler**
- **Clear eye-ring**

69

? ✓ Were its throat and breast greyish brown?

? ✓ Did it have a black cap?

? ✓ Was its back brown?

? ✓ Was it greyish brown underneath?

I saw this bird on (date)

....

at (time)

....

It was (activity)

....

my notes

_____

_____

_____

_____

_____

my pictures

my observations

Black Cap (*Sylvia atricapilla*)

The black cap belongs to the warbler family, and shares the warblers' talent for song. In the spring it can be seen and heard singing from a high perch, often an oak tree. Black caps and garden warblers are often seen working their way through brambles and undergrowth together. Although mainly an insect-eater, the black cap is an enthusiastic berry- and fruit-eater in the autumn. Increasing numbers of black caps are overwintering in Britain, and these are appearing at the bird-table during winter months. In the garden the black cap can be quite aggressive when competing for scraps, often frightening off much larger birds.

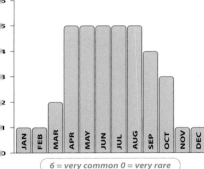

6 = very common 0 = very rare

FACTS

SIZE	Length 13–15 cm Weight 14–20 g	
COLOUR	MALE: Grey-brown upperparts. Grey underparts. Distinctive black cap ending at eye-level. FEMALE: Brown-buff underparts and red-brown cap. WINTER DIFFERENCES: None.	
NEST	Grass, roots, hair lining. In thick undergrowth, brambles, bushes.	
CALL	'Tak' when disturbed. Song – loud and warbling.	

RESIDENT/VISITOR
Summer visitor from the Mediterranean and North Africa. Increasing number of winter residents.

👁 QUICK IDENTIFICATION

- Male's black cap, ending at eye-level
- Female's bright red-brown cap
- Aggressive bird-table behaviour
- Tendency to puff out feathers when cold

black cap

grey-brown upperparts

notched tail

♂

? ✓ Was its body shaped like a torpedo?

? ✓ Was its tail short and forked?

? ✓ Was its voice like a high-pitched scream?

? ✓ Did it look like a swallow?

I saw this bird on (date)

....

at (time)

....

It was (activity)

....

my notes

_____

_____

_____

_____

_____

my pictures

Swift *(Apus apus)*

The swifts we see and hear in our skies have probably been hatched here, but they spend over half of the year in Africa. The swift is an extraordinary bird, which spends practically all its life in the air. Living on flying insects and floating spiders caught in midair, the swift feeds, sleeps, and even sometimes mates on the wing. It lands to build its nest, lay and hatch its eggs, and care for the young until they leave the nest. When the young do finally leave the nest, they are likely to stay airborne for the next two or three years.

JAN	
FEB	
MAR	
APR	
MAY	
JUN	
JUL	
AUG	
SEP	
OCT	
NOV	
DEC	

6 = very common 0 = very rare

RESIDENT/VISITOR
Arrives in May from Africa. Leaves early August.

FACTS

SIZE	Length 16.4 cm Weight 45 g
COLOUR	MALE: Dull brown all over, apart from light patch under chin. FEMALE: Same as male. WINTER DIFFERENCES: None.
NEST	Straw, feathers, plant-down collected in midair, bound together with saliva. Sited in holes in trees, caves, buildings. Will accept a suitable nest-box.
CALL	Shrill 'swee-ree', emitted much of the time. Female call has higher pitch.

👁 QUICK IDENTIFICATION

- **Long, narrow, sickle-shaped wings**
- **Regular screaming call**
- **All-over dark colouring**
- **Flying style of fast flap and long glide**

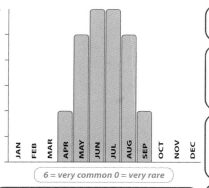

all-black colouration

♂♀

long, narrow wings

73

? ✓ Did it have a deeply forked tail?

? ✓ Was it flying acrobatically?

? ✓ Was the top of the bird blue-black in colour?

? ✓ Were its wings long and angled?

I saw this bird on (date)

....

at (time)

....

It was (activity)

....

my notes

_____

_____

_____

_____

_____

my pictures

my observations

Swallow *(Hirundo rustica)*

Once a cliff nester, the swallow now prefers to build its nest in and around human habitation. It is a low flier, skimming the surface of rivers and ponds to catch insects in its gaping bill, or snatch a drink on the wing. The swallow is a fine navigator, and often returns to the same nest-site for several years. Unlike the swift, the swallow can perch without problems on wires and buildings. It rarely lands on the ground, except to collect mud for nest building. Swallows are social birds, often roosting together in hundreds in reed-beds. Swallows gathering on telephone wires before returning south are a familiar sight.

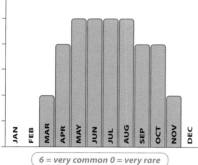

6 = very common 0 = very rare

RESIDENT/VISITOR
A summer visitor, arriving as early as late March. Returns to sub-Saharan Africa in September or October.

FACTS

SIZE	Length 19 cm Weight 20 g
COLOUR	MALE: Dark, glossy blue upperparts, head and upper breast. Dark red forehead, chin and throat. White to creamy underparts. FEMALE: Similar to male, though a little duller. WINTER DIFFERENCES: None.
NEST	NEST: Shallow cup-shaped, mud and dry grass, cemented with saliva. On ledges and rafters in barns, stables and other buildings. Often in colonies.
CALL	'Tswit-tswit'. Alarm call is a high 'tswee'.

👁 QUICK IDENTIFICATION

- **Long tail streamers**
- **Red head and throat**
- **Dark blue breast band**
- **Low-level flight in straight lines**

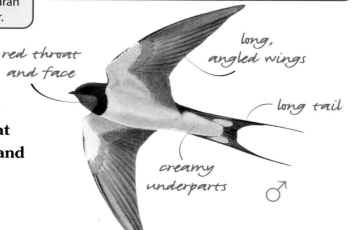

red throat and face

long, angled wings

long tail

creamy underparts ♂

? ✓ Did it have a white chin and rump?

? ✓ Was its tail short and forked?

? ✓ Was its head blue-black?

? ✓ Were its wings black?

I saw this bird on (date)

....

at (time)

....

It was (activity)

....

my notes

_____

_____

_____

_____

_____

my pictures

my observations

House Martin (Delichon urbica)

The house martin has developed a closer connection with human habitation than even the swallow. It builds its unique mud nest close under the eaves on the outsides of buildings. It is a social bird, and often nests in colonies. The house martin lives on a diet of flying insects caught in midair. It has a streamlined body and is a powerful and agile flier, though it flutters more than a swallow. It can land on the ground, where it collects mud for its nest-building. House martin pairs bring up two or three broods per year, and sometimes young birds from the first brood help to feed birds from later broods.

6 = very common 0 = very rare

RESIDENT/VISITOR
Summer visitor, arriving in April from sub-Saharan Africa, and returning in September or October.

FACTS

SIZE	Length 12.5 cm Weight 18 g
COLOUR	MALE: Blue-black above. White chin, throat, underparts and rump. Dark grey wings and tail. Short white leg feathers. FEMALE: Same as male. WINTER DIFFERENCES: None.
NEST	A mud and feathers cup with a small entrance hole is constructed under building eaves.
CALL	'Tsrr'. Alarm call 'sier – sier'.

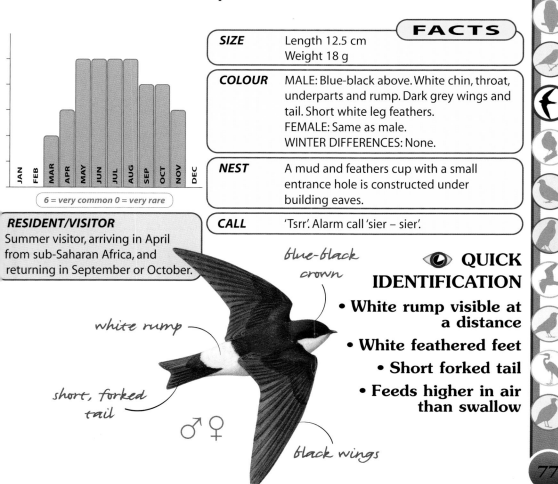

blue-black crown

white rump

short, forked tail

♂ ♀

black wings

QUICK IDENTIFICATION

- **White rump visible at a distance**
- **White feathered feet**
- **Short forked tail**
- **Feeds higher in air than swallow**

? ✓ Did it run along the ground with its tail wagging?

? ✓ Did it have a long, notched tail?

? ✓ Was it black and white?

? ✓ Did it have a black bib?

I saw this bird on (date)

....

at (time)

....

It was (activity)

....

my notes

_____

_____

_____

_____

_____

my pictures

my observations

Pied Wagtail *(Motacilla alba)*

The pied wagtail always seems to be in a hurry, running over the ground in fast bursts, stopping, wagging its tail up and down, then running on. All the time it is looking for insects, frequently stabbing at the ground or leaping into the air to capture a tidbit. It comes to the bird-table, usually picking up what other birds have dropped on the ground. The pied wagtail is found across the country, and likes foraging at the edge of water where there is plenty of insect life. In the evening it flies to roost, with hundreds of others, in reeds and bushes.

JAN FEB MAR APR MAY JUN JUL AUG SEP OCT NOV DEC

6 = very common 0 = very rare

RESIDENT/VISITOR
Resident, though some move further south in the country in winter, and some continue on as far as the Mediterranean.

FACTS

SIZE	Length 18 cm Weight 22 g
COLOUR	MALE: White forehead and face. Black crown, throat, upper breast, back, tail. Outer wing and outer tail feathers white. Underparts white. FEMALE: Greyer back. Smaller bib. WINTER DIFFERENCES: Greyer back and white throat. Black breast crescent.
NEST	Cup-shaped, made of dry grass, and lined with rootlets and hair. Low in bushes, including rhododendrons, and brambles.
CALL	'Tu-reep' and 'tchisseek'.

👁 QUICK IDENTIFICATION

Runs in short, fast bursts

Tail wags up and down

Wave-like, swooping flight

Black and white plumage

black crown, throat and upper breast

white-tipped flight feathers

white face

long, notched tail

♂

? Was it perched in an upright position? ✓

? Did it have a short, broad bill? ✓

? Was its breast speckled? ✓

? Did it have a streaked crown? ✓

I saw this bird on (date)

....

at (time)

....

It was (activity)

....

my notes

_____

_____

_____

_____

my pictures

my observations

Spotted Flycatcher *(Muscicapa striata)*

The spotted flycatcher is interested in all flying insects, from butterflies to wasps. When it catches something with a sting, it batters it against its perch until it is no longer a threat. Males and females usually feed separately, and hunting is done from a perch such as a stump. The spotted flycatcher is an ambush-hunter, patiently sitting on its observation perch for long stretches, then suddenly darting off to seize a passing insect, and returning to the perch to deal with it. Its favourite hunting-grounds are wood margins and clearings, overgrown gardens, parkland and beside water. It is often found near human habitation.

JAN FEB MAR APR MAY JUN JUL AUG SEP OCT NOV DEC

6 = very common 0 = very rare

RESIDENT/VISITOR
Summer visitor, arriving in May from Africa, returning in July to September.

FACTS

SIZE	Length 14 cm Weight 15–16 g
COLOUR	MALE: Grey-brown upper plumage. Off-white underparts with grey streaks. Streaked forehead and breast. FEMALE: Same as male. WINTER DIFFERENCES: None.
NEST	Untidy – moss, wool, hair, bound with cobwebs. On a ledge in creeper on wall or tree. On a bough or a beam. In an old nest of another bird.
CALL	'Tsee' and 'tzek-tuk-tuk'.

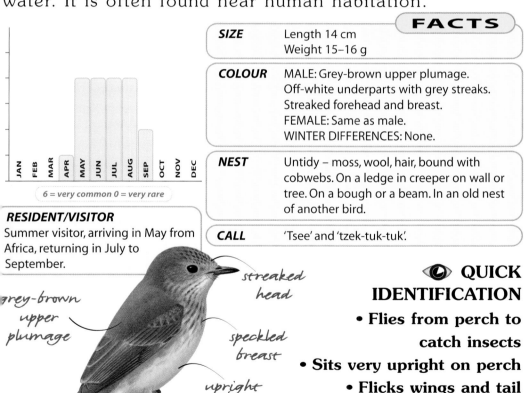

grey-brown upper plumage

streaked head

speckled breast

upright posture

♂ ♀

👁 QUICK IDENTIFICATION

- **Flies from perch to catch insects**
- **Sits very upright on perch**
- **Flicks wings and tail when calling**
- **Lightly streaked, off-white breast**

81

? ✓   Did it have a red face and breast?

? ✓   Did it have a high-pitched, sweet song?

? ✓   Was the rest of the bird light brown?

? ✓   Was its belly white?

I saw this bird on (date)

13.3.12

at (time)

08:15

It was (activity)

feeding

my notes

my pictures

my observations

Robin *(Erithacus rubecula)*

Probably Britain's most easily recognized bird, the robin is perfectly at home in the garden. It is famous for boldly coming close to anyone digging, in the hope of catching worms and grubs that are dug up. The robin sings to establish its territorial boundaries, and attract mates. It defends its territory with extreme aggression, and has even been known to fight to the death. In very harsh weather robins may observe a temporary truce, and you could see several feeding together at the bird-table. Unafraid of humans, they rapidly become almost hand-tame when provided with regular food.

JAN FEB MAR APR MAY JUN JUL AUG SEP OCT NOV DEC

6 = very common 0 = very rare

RESIDENT/VISITOR
Resident. Joined by paler-coloured visitors from northern Europe in winter.

FACTS

SIZE	Length 14 cm Weight 16–22 g
COLOUR	MALE: Light brown crown, back, tail and wings. Face and breast bright orange-red. Undersides white with buff tinge, with bands of white extending round the red breast, up and over the eyes. FEMALE: Same as male. WINTER DIFFERENCES: None.
NEST	Domed, made of grass, wool, moss, hair. In hole in bank or wall. Sometimes in sheds, in old buckets and other containers.
CALL	'Tik-tik'. Sweet, high-pitched twittery song.

👁 QUICK IDENTIFICATION

- **Perky shape and red breast**
- **Great territorial aggression, especially in spring**
- **Bold approach to humans**
- **Fluffed out almost spherical in cold weather**

white eye-rings

red face and breast

white belly

♂♀

? ✓ Was it flitting and hopping about?

? ✓ Did it have a cocked tail?

? ✓ Did it have barred markings on its back, wings and tail?

? ✓ Was it small and round?

I saw this bird on (date)

....

at (time)

....

It was (activity)

....

my notes

my pictures

my observations

Wren *(Troglodytes troglodytes)*

The tiny wren features in many folk tales. It is a resident species and is found in most terrains except the centres of large cities. This common garden bird has fast movements and a whirring flight. The male makes several nests at the beginning of the breeding season, and the female chooses which one to line and use for laying her eggs. The wren eats mainly larvae and spiders as well as some seeds. Like other very small birds, it sometimes nests with others in winter to keep warm. More than 60 have been known to cram into a single nest-box. Sometimes as much as 70 percent of the wren population fails to survive a harsh winter.

FACTS

SIZE	Length 9.5 cm Weight 9 g
COLOUR	MALE: Russet-brown mantle, with darker bars. Wings, tail and flanks distinctly barred. Lighter underparts. Cream stripe over eye. FEMALE: Same as male. WINTER DIFFERENCES: None.
NEST	Moss, grass, bracken, local materials. Domed shape. In banks, piles of wood, thickets, walls, tree roots.
CALL	'Tek – tek' and 'tsrr'. Loud, trilling song – some notes too high for human hearing.

6 = very common 0 = very rare

RESIDENT/VISITOR
Resident.

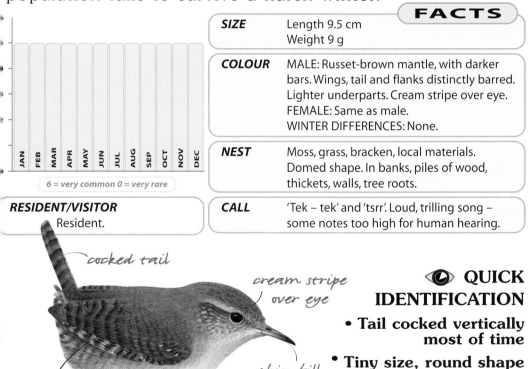

cocked tail

cream stripe over eye

thin bill

barred pattern on wings and tail

♂ ♀

👁 QUICK IDENTIFICATION

- Tail cocked vertically most of time
- Tiny size, round shape
- Mouse-like movements through hedge bottoms
- Thin, insect-eater's bill

85

? Was it a large bird?

? Did it have a pink breast?

? Was there a shiny patch on its neck?

? Did it make a repetitive coo call?

I saw this bird on (date)

....

at (time)

....

It was (activity)

....

my notes

my pictures

my observations

Woodpigeon *(Columba palumbus)*

The impressive size of the woodpigeon clearly marks it out from others in the dove and pigeon family. Its take-off is a startling clatter of wings, and it is a powerful flier. With populations in both town and country, the woodpigeon is mainly a ground feeder, but it prefers an environment with plenty of trees in which to perch and nest. It feeds on plant material, seeds and berries, including crops such as peas and beans. It will visit the bird-table, but is a nuisance in the vegetable garden, where it specializes in devouring young plants of the cabbage family, as well as soft fruit.

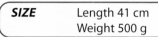

JAN FEB MAR APR MAY JUN JUL AUG SEP OCT NOV DEC

6 = very common 0 = very rare

RESIDENT/VISITOR
Resident.

FACTS

SIZE	Length 41 cm Weight 500 g
COLOUR	MALE: Blue-grey head. Greeny-blue nape. White patches on side of neck. Pale salmon throat and breast. Buff wings with a white band. Dark grey outer wing feathers. FEMALE: Smaller neck patches. Pale grey tail with dark tip. WINTER DIFFERENCES: None.
NEST	A few twigs. In trees, hedgerows, old nests. Ledges on town buildings.
CALL	'Coo-COOO-coo, coo-coo'.

👁 QUICK IDENTIFICATION

- **Large size, long tail**
- **White neck patches**
- **White wing band in flight**
- **Noisy, clattering escape flight**

shiny patch

white patch

grey upperparts

short, red legs

♂

? ☑ Did it have a white rump?

? ☑ Were its legs short and pink?

? ☑ Did it walk along the ground?

? ☑ Was it large and mainly grey?

I saw this bird on (date)

....

at (time)

....

It was (activity)

....

my notes

_____

_____

_____

_____

_____

my pictures

Feral Pigeon/Rock Dove (Columba livia)

Seen everywhere from wheat fields to city squares, the feral pigeon is descended from the rock dove. This was specially bred to provide food and racing birds, and then reverted to the wild. It has interbred widely, and has a large variety of colours and markings. The wild rock dove still lives on and around northern sea cliffs. Feral pigeons colonize all human environments, including railway stations, public buildings and blocks of flats. They nest on ledges and feed on whatever they can find. They also feed in flocks in the countryside. The rock dove feeds on seeds and plant material in fields and woods. It perches on rocks or the ground rather than in trees.

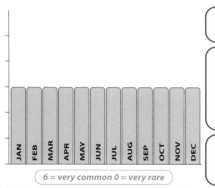

JAN FEB MAR APR MAY JUN JUL AUG SEP OCT NOV DEC

6 = very common 0 = very rare

RESIDENT/VISITOR
Resident.

FACTS

SIZE	Length 31–34 cm Weight 250–350 g
COLOUR	MALE: Bluish body. Light grey back and wings. Double dark wing bars. Metallic green and purple neck. White rump and underwing. FEMALE: Same as male. WINTER DIFFERENCES: None.
NEST	Rock dove's nest: roots, seaweed, heather, on rocky ledge. Urban feral pigeons nest on building ledges and in niches.
CALL	'Ruh-ruh-ruh'.

QUICK IDENTIFICATION

- **White underwings and rump**
- **Double wing bars**
- **No black on wing tips**
- **Flies low over water**

dark wing bars

black and white bill

♂♀

grey underparts

pink, short legs

? ✓ Did it have a tail with a dark black banded tip?

? ✓ Was its breast pinkish?

? ✓ Did it have a turquoise-green neck patch?

? ✓ Did it have tiny, black wing bars?

I saw this bird on (date)

....

at (time)

....

It was (activity)

....

my notes

_____

_____

_____

_____

_____

my pictures

my observations

Stock Dove *(Columba oenas)*

More solitary than woodpigeons, stock doves can sometimes be seen feeding alongside them in the winter. Found everywhere in Britain except the extreme north of Scotland, the stock dove's habitats include woods, rocky coasts, dunes, cliffs and parkland. It occasionally eats snails and larvae, but most of its food is vegetable, including leaves, crops such as beans and corn, clover, seeds, buds and flowers. The stock dove has an impressive display flight in the breeding season when both male and female fly around in circles, gliding with raised wings, and performing wing 'clapping'. On the ground they go through bowing ceremonies.

6 = very common 0 = very rare

RESIDENT/VISITOR
Resident.

FACTS

SIZE	Length 32–34 cm Weight 290–330 g
COLOUR	MALE: Purplish blue head, body and wings. Dark edges to wings, plus two small dark bars. Glossy turquoise-green nape. Rosy breast. Broad band at end of tail. FEMALE: Upperparts have a brownish tinge. WINTER DIFFERENCES: None.
NEST	Roots and twigs. In holes in trees, cliffs, caves, rabbit burrows. Sometimes no nesting material used.
CALL	'OOO-roo-oo'.

👁 QUICK IDENTIFICATION

- **Absence of any white on plumage**
- **Loud, rhythmic, booming call**
- **Two small wing bars and dark edges to wings**
- **Two black spots on wings seen in flight**

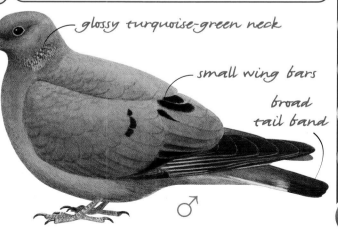

glossy turquoise-green neck

small wing bars

broad tail band

♂

? ✓ Did it have a repeated coo-cooo-coo call?

? ✓ Did it have a black collar, edged with white?

? ✓ Was its tail tipped with white underneath?

? ✓ Were its legs red?

I saw this bird on (date)

....

at (time)

....

It was (activity)

....

my notes

_____

_____

_____

_____

_____

my pictures

my observations

Collared Dove (*Streptopelia decaocto*)

The collared dove has become common in Britain only in the last 50 years, having migrated from India via Europe. This bird stays close to human society, and benefits in several ways. It feeds alongside farm poultry and cattle, sharing in their meals, and also hangs around sites such as docks, breweries, stables and zoos where there is grain to be found. It is seen in both towns and villages, and soon finds the local bird-tables, turning up regularly for seeds and scraps. Where food is plentiful, the collared dove may feed in sizable flocks, especially in winter. It eats snails and insects as well as seeds.

FACTS

SIZE	Length 28–32 cm Weight 200 g
COLOUR	MALE: Pale fawn-grey all over. Pinker tinge to underparts. Black half-collar at back of neck. Dark grey wing tips. Black bar under tail and white tip. FEMALE: Similar to male. WINTER DIFFERENCES: None.
NEST	Loose platform of sticks, grass, roots. On buildings, in trees (preferably conifers), sometimes on ground.
CALL	Deep 'coo-coooo, coo'. 'Hwee' in flight.

JAN FEB MAR APR MAY JUN JUL AUG SEP OCT NOV DEC

6 = very common 0 = very rare

RESIDENT/VISITOR
Resident.

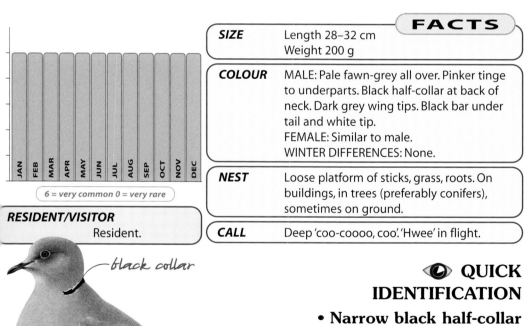

black collar

fawny-grey wings

pinkish breast

white undertail

♂ ♀

👁 QUICK IDENTIFICATION

- **Narrow black half-collar**
- **Black base under tail in flight**
- **All-over pale colouring**
- **Slimmer than pigeons**

93

? ✓ Did it have a long, four-barred tail?

? ✓ Was it alone?

? ✓ Did it have a distinctive kek-kek-kek call?

? ✓ Was its throat white?

I saw this bird on (date)

....

at (time)

....

It was (activity)

....

my notes

_____

_____

_____

_____

_____

my pictures

my observations

Sparrowhawk *(Accipiter nisus)*

Sparrowhawks are becoming more common in large gardens, which is unfortunate for most visitors to the bird-table, as the sparrowhawk specializes in catching small birds on the wing. When hunting, this smallish predator flies low over bushes and hedges, flapping and gliding, and weaves between tree-trunks, catching its prey by surprise. The female, as in many birds of prey, is considerably larger than the male, and twice his weight. Once severely reduced in numbers due to the use of agricultural pesticides, the sparrowhawk now appears to be making a come-back.

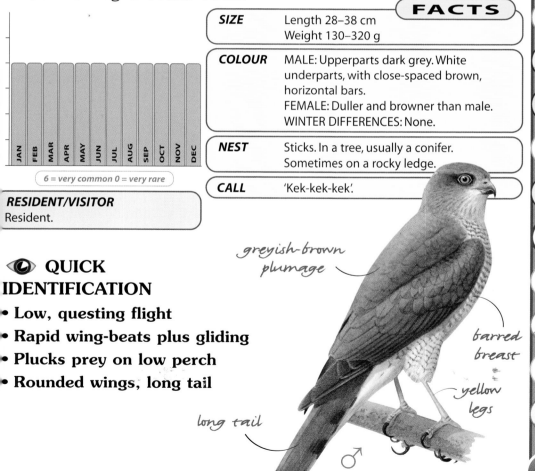

greyish-brown plumage

barred breast

yellow legs

long tail

♂

FACTS

SIZE	Length 28–38 cm Weight 130–320 g
COLOUR	MALE: Upperparts dark grey. White underparts, with close-spaced brown, horizontal bars. FEMALE: Duller and browner than male. WINTER DIFFERENCES: None.
NEST	Sticks. In a tree, usually a conifer. Sometimes on a rocky ledge.
CALL	'Kek-kek-kek'.

JAN FEB MAR APR MAY JUN JUL AUG SEP OCT NOV DEC

6 = very common 0 = very rare

RESIDENT/VISITOR
Resident.

👁 QUICK IDENTIFICATION

- Low, questing flight
- Rapid wing-beats plus gliding
- Plucks prey on low perch
- Rounded wings, long tail

? ✓ Was it about 35 cm long?

? ✓ Did it have red legs and a red bill?

? ✓ Did you see its winter white head or summer dark head?

? ✓ Did it have black wing-tips?

I saw this bird on (date)
....

at (time)
....

It was (activity)
....

my notes

my pictures

my observations

Black-headed Gull (*Larus ridibundus*)

This elegant little gull is an enthusiastic inland forager, which sometimes swoops to grab food from the bird-table, but more usually is seen around rubbish dumps and ploughed fields. The black-headed gull is the commonest gull found inland, and feeds on insects, worms and snails, as well as waste scraps and carrion. It is also common in its more natural habitat of coasts, harbours, low shores and estuaries, where fish figures more in its diet. It is fond of swimming, and outside the breeding season sometimes comes into large cities, particularly those on rivers.

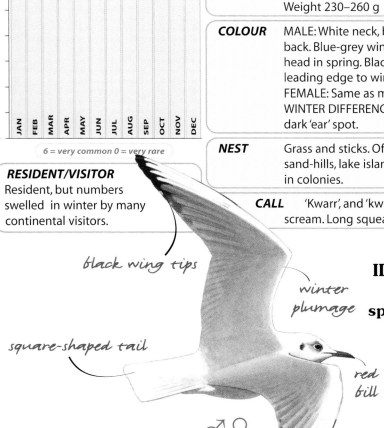

JAN FEB MAR APR MAY JUN JUL AUG SEP OCT NOV DEC

6 = very common 0 = very rare

RESIDENT/VISITOR
Resident, but numbers swelled in winter by many continental visitors.

FACTS

SIZE	Length 35–38 cm Weight 230–260 g
COLOUR	MALE: White neck, breast, underparts and back. Blue-grey wings. Chocolate-brown head in spring. Black wing-tips. White leading edge to wings. FEMALE: Same as male. WINTER DIFFERENCES: White head, with dark 'ear' spot.
NEST	Grass and sticks. Often in marsh, also sand-hills, lake islands, shingle. Nests in colonies.
CALL	'Kwarr', and 'kwwup', plus a raucous scream. Long squealing calls.

black wing tips

winter plumage

square-shaped tail

red bill

♂ ♀

👁 QUICK IDENTIFICATION

- **Dark head in spring and summer**
- **Small size, slim shape**
- **Deep red bill and legs**
- **White leading edge to wings**

? ✓ Did it look rather like a rook?

? ✓ Was it completely black all over?

? ✓ Did it have a short, heavy black bill?

? ✓ Did it make a loud kaaw sound?

I saw this bird on (date)

....

at (time)

....

It was (activity)

....

my notes

my pictures

my observations

Carrion Crow *(Corvus corone)*

The carrion crow feeds on dead animals (carrion means dead flesh), but will also kill small creatures such as mice and voles. It also steals both eggs and nestlings from small birds' nests. It is at home in the town as well as the countryside, and builds its nest in parks, squares and large gardens with mature trees. The carrion crow's powerful, curved beak is designed for tearing flesh, and sheep farmers claim that it attacks lambs or trapped sheep. On the coast it is known for cracking open crabs and shellfish by dropping them from a height onto rocks and roads.

JAN FEB MAR APR MAY JUN JUL AUG SEP OCT NOV DEC

6 = very common 0 = very rare

FACTS

SIZE	Length 47 cm Weight 550 g
COLOUR	MALE: Glossy black all over, with a black bill. FEMALE: Same as male. WINTER DIFFERENCES: None.
NEST	Twigs. High in a tree fork, or on a cliff ledge. In bushes in hill country.
CALL	Deep, drawn-out 'kaaw'.

RESIDENT/VISITOR
Resident. Some carrion crows come as winter visitors from the continent.

all over
black plumage

short,
heavy
bill

👁 **QUICK IDENTIFICATION**

- **All black colouring including beak**
- **Much smaller than raven**
- **Neat, smooth plumage**
- **Nests singly, not in colonies**

♂♀

? ✓ Did it look like a smaller crow or rook?

? ✓ Was the nape of its neck grey?

? ✓ Did it have a white eye-ring?

? ✓ Were its legs black?

I saw this bird on (date)

....

at (time)

....

It was (activity)

....

my notes

my pictures

my observations

Jackdaw *(Corvus monedula)*

The jackdaw is a sociable bird, nesting in colonies in a variety of sites, including church towers, cliffs, ancient ruins and woodland trees. It also feeds in flocks in open countryside, moving rapidly over the ground looking for insects, caterpillars, worms and snails. The jackdaw happily invades the bird-table, and will eat practically anything on offer, including seeds, scraps and cheese. Quicker and more agile than most members of the crow family, it can often be seen in mixed feeding flocks which include rooks and starlings. During its mating rituals, the jackdaw raises its crown feathers and displays its silver-grey hood.

JAN FEB MAR APR MAY JUN JUL AUG SEP OCT NOV DEC

6 = very common 0 = very rare

RESIDENT/VISITOR
Resident. Some birds move west in winter, as far as Ireland in some cases. There are also winter visitors from the Continent.

FACTS

SIZE	Length 33 cm Weight 220–270 g
COLOUR	MALE: Black with a blue gloss. Ash-grey neck, nape and back of head. Black crown. FEMALE: Same as male. WINTER DIFFERENCES: None.
NEST	Twigs, with grass, wool and hair lining. In trees, rocky crevices, buildings, old nests, burrows. In colonies.
CALL	'Chuck-chuck' and 'chiup' danger call.

QUICK IDENTIFICATION

- **Ash-grey head with black crown**
- **Piercing eyes with pale blue irises**
- **Quick ground movements**
- **Agile flight**

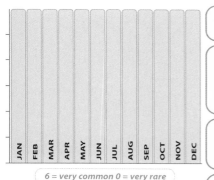

grey nape of neck

white eye-ring

black plumage

♂ ♀

? ☑ Was it mainly black and white?

? ☑ Did it have a long greenish-black tail?

? ☑ Were its wings blue-black?

? ☑ Was its bill short, black and thin?

I saw this bird on (date)

....

at (time)

....

It was (activity)

....

my notes

my pictures

my observations

Magpie *(Pica pica)*

The subject of many country superstitions, the magpie is unmistakable with its contrasting plumage, long tail and loud voice. It is seen in town and country, and eats everything from berries, fruit, nuts, peas and grain to large table scraps and baby birds. Magpies are usually seen in pairs or small groups. It is often unwelcome in gardens with nest-boxes, but is, in fact, far less of a problem for fledglings than the domestic cat. It is unpopular with gamekeepers who wage war on it for taking pheasant eggs. Like other crows, the magpie sometimes buries surplus food to eat later. It also likes to bury shiny objects, and, along with the jackdaw, has a largely undeserved reputation as a jewel thief.

6 = very common 0 = very rare

RESIDENT/VISITOR
Resident.

FACTS

SIZE	Length 40–46 cm Weight 200–250 g
COLOUR	MALE: White shoulders, flanks and belly. Black head, bill, upper breast and cape. Greenish shiny tail feathers with purple tips. Glossy blue-black wings. FEMALE: Same as male. WINTER DIFFERENCES: None.
NEST	Large domed structure of twigs. Roots and earth lining. In trees and hedgerows.
CALL	Harsh 'chak-ak-ak-ak'.

👁 QUICK IDENTIFICATION

- **Contrasting black and white plumage**
- **Very long, graduated tail**
- **Loud, repeated call**
- **Noisy groups in winter**

blue-black wings

long greenish-black tail

♂ ♀

103

? ☑ Did it have blue and white patches on its wings?

? ☑ Did it have a black and white streaked head?

? ☑ Was its breast pinkish brown?

? ☑ Did it have a black moustache?

I saw this bird on (date)

....

at (time)

....

It was (activity)

....

my notes

_____

_____

_____

_____

_____

my pictures

my observations

Jay (Garrulus glandarius)

The jay, despite its colourful plumage, is a member of the crow family. It is a shy bird. However, it has become bolder as it moves into suburban areas. It will come to the bird-table, usually early in the morning, before humans are about. It is fond of peanuts, and shakes them to the ground from their suspended nets. The jay likes acorns, and sometimes hides them and beech mast in the ground. In the countryside, as well as eating wild foods, the jay readily tucks into cultivated crops such as peas and corn. It also eats animal prey, including mice, small birds and their eggs, and insects.

	FACTS
SIZE	Length 34 cm Weight 140–190 g
COLOUR	MALE: Body pinkish brown. White rump. Black tail. White wing patches. Blue and black wing bars. Black and white crown feathers. Black moustache. FEMALE: Same as male. WINTER DIFFERENCES: None.
NEST	Twigs and earth, lined with roots and hair. Low in a tree.
CALL	Harsh 'skraak'.

JAN FEB MAR APR MAY JUN JUL AUG SEP OCT NOV DEC

6 = very common 0 = very rare

RESIDENT/VISITOR
Resident.

streaked crown

black moustache

brownish pink

blue patches

♂ ♀

👁 **QUICK IDENTIFICATION**
- Pinkish body, blue wing bars
- Loud, harsh call
- White rump and black tail in flight
- Black and white crown feathers,

? Was it slimmer than a crow?

? Did it have a bare area above its bill?

? Was it black all over?

? Did it have a cawing 'kaah' call?

I saw this bird on (date)

....

at (time)

....

It was (activity)

....

my notes

my pictures

my observations

Rook (Corvus frugilegus)

Rookeries, high in the tops of clumps of trees, are particularly noisy in spring, when the rooks quarrel over nest-sites and go through their mating displays. The rook is the best-known British social bird, living in large colonies of nests, and travelling in flocks between the rookery and the feeding-grounds. The rook flies with a leisurely, slow, flapping and gliding flight. It feeds on pests such as caterpillars, snails, wire worms and beetle larvae, but the farmer only notices the grain it also takes. Occasionally it is attracted to garden bird-tables when bones and fat are put out.

JAN FEB MAR APR MAY JUN JUL AUG SEP OCT NOV DEC

6 = very common 0 = very rare

FACTS

SIZE	Length 46 cm Weight 480 g
COLOUR	MALE: glossy black plumage with a blue-green tint. Whitish featherless skin at the base of the bill. FEMALE: Same as male. WINTER DIFFERENCES: None.
NEST	Twigs, earth, lined with grass, moss, dead leaves. In tree-tops in a colony.
CALL	Deep 'kaah'.

RESIDENT/VISITOR
Resident. Some continental migrants overwinter in Britain.

👁 QUICK IDENTIFICATION

- Bare, whitish base to bill
- Ragged-looking breast and leg feathers
- High crown and long bill
- Very noisy social groups

bare face above thin, grey bill

slimmer than the crow

♂♀

? ✓ Did it have a long, white neck?

? ✓ Did it have a black crest?

? ✓ Were its back and wings grey?

? ✓ Did it have long, yellow legs?

I saw this bird on (date)
....

at (time)
....

It was (activity)
....

my notes

my pictures

my observations

Grey Heron (Ardea cinerea)

The stately grey heron is found all over the British Isles, and is a familiar sight standing patiently in marshes and the shallows of lakes and rivers. It either stalks its prey with very slow movements, or waits motionless in order to surprise it with a sudden strike of its powerful, pointed beak. Its prey is usually fish, but it also catches frogs, worms, insects and small mammals. Usually the only time it appears in the garden is when it drops in to clear out the resident goldfish from the garden pond. The grey heron lives in colonies in the canopies of tall trees.

JAN FEB MAR APR MAY JUN JUL AUG SEP OCT NOV DEC

6 = very common 0 = very rare

RESIDENT/VISITOR
Resident.

FACTS

SIZE	Length 90–98 cm Weight 1.1–1.7 kg
COLOUR	MALE: Grey wings and back. White neck and head. Black eye-stripe and neck markings. Long black feathers protruding from back of head. Black tips and trailing edges to wings. Yellow bill. FEMALE: Same as male. WINTER DIFFERENCES: None.
NEST	Large, built of sticks in tree-top colony.
CALL	'Kraak', and 'krreik' in flight.

👁 QUICK IDENTIFICATION

- **Very lank, long-legged shape**
- **S-shaped kinked neck in flight**
- **Heavy, pointed yellow bill**
- **Stands in shallows fishing**

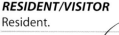
black crest

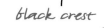

white neck with black stripe

orange-yellow legs

♂ ♀

? ✓ Did the bird have a red area around its eyes?

? ✓ Was the tail long, barred black, pointed and brown?

? ✓ Was its crown green?

? ✓ Did it fly quite low?

my notes

I saw this bird on (date)

....

at (time)

....

It was (activity)

....

my pictures

my observations

Common Pheasant (Phasianus colchicus)

Introduced centuries ago from Asia as a game bird, most pheasants are reared in controlled areas for shooting. However, many also live outside the artificial breeding pens. The pheasant has adapted well to the European woodlands. When alarmed it usually runs from danger, crouching low to the ground, but if approached too closely, erupts into the air with a startling clatter of wings before flying and gliding to safety. Due to unnaturally high numbers of birds bred for hunting, pheasants are frequent road casualties. A ground forager, the pheasant is often seen at the edge of woods, on farmland, and in parks and large gardens.

JAN FEB MAR APR MAY JUN JUL AUG SEP OCT NOV DEC

6 = very common 0 = very rare

RESIDENT/VISITOR
Resident.

👁 QUICK IDENTIFICATION

Loud territorial and alarm calls

Red wattles and feather 'ears' of male

Long tail, especially male

Clattering take-off

FACTS	
SIZE	Length 53–89 cm Weight 1–1.2 kg
COLOUR	MALE: Red area around eyes. Neck and crown dark metallic green. White neck-ring. Ruddy brown plumage with horizontal lines of black 'scale' markings. Dark bars on tail. FEMALE: Light brown, with dark brown 'scale' markings. No wattles. WINTER DIFFERENCES: None.
NEST	Hollow in the ground, lined with grass and leaves. Hidden in brambles, ferns, reeds, woodland undergrowth.
CALL	Loud 'kuk-kuk' plus whirr of wings when male proclaims territory. 'Tsik-tsik' by disturbed female. 'Gug-gug-gug' – taking off in alarm.

coppery coloured plumage

red wattle

♂

long, barred pattern tail

INDEX

Cover photograph of Chaffinch by Roger Wilmshurst/FLPA